UNRAVELING THE TAPESTRY OF DYSFUNCTION

A Common Thread In Every Family

Mable Alyse Manning

Published And Distributed By
Mable Alyse Publishing
Los Angeles, California
Email: manningalyse@gmail.com
Website: mablealyse.com

Packaging/Consulting
Professional Publishing House
1425 W. Manchester Ave. Ste B
Los Angeles, California 90047
323-750-3592
Email: professionalpublishinghouse@yahoo.com
www.Professionalpublishinghouse.com

Cover design: TWA Solutions
First printing March 2024
ISBN: 979-8-218-40336-2
10987654321

Dedication

I dedicate this book to those who have experienced the unique journey of growing up with siblings. The gift of family is immeasurable. Sharing a home with loved ones creates lasting memories. Watching families navigate through disagreements and dynamics is part of life's tapestry. Regrettably, many families face dysfunction, and not everyone feels gratitude for their familial upbringing. It's a wish for some to have chosen a different path. Although we can't choose our families, they shape us. Despite dysfunction, the family remains our core unit.

Regardless of our family's challenges, they profoundly influence who we are. I hope this book serves families worldwide, offering solace in the shared experience. May you find peace, healing, and reconciliation within your family dynamics. Let forgiveness initiate the way toward harmony. Life is fleeting; express your love to your family daily.

Table of Contents

Foreword

In *Unraveling the Tapestry of Dysfunction*, Mable Alyse Manning exposes the pervasive nature of family dysfunction, transcending class, and economic barriers. Building on the success of her previous work, Manning offers practical insights to help readers recognize and confront dysfunction within their own families. Through compassionate guidance, she empowers individuals to break free from destructive patterns and seek professional support without shame or guilt. This transformative book is a beacon of hope for those seeking healing and reconciliation within their families.

This timely literary work reminds us that while we cannot choose our family, we hold the power to rewrite its narrative and embark on a journey of healing and restoration.

Dr. Rosie Milligan
Minister, Author, Publisher, Talk Show Host, and
Founder of Black Writers On Tour.

Prelude

Dysfunction permeates every family, transcending social status and geographical boundaries. From east to west, across cities, states, and homes, dysfunction manifests itself universally. Regardless of nationality, dysfunction is a ubiquitous reality. Even esteemed institutions like the White House and Buckingham Palace, down to impoverished communities, grapple with family discord. No family is immune. We must all learn how to halt the unraveling of the family's tapestry. It's ironic that while members often acknowledge dysfunction, many opt to ignore it, and some perpetuate the cycle by disregarding it altogether. Astonishingly, many families normalize dysfunction, hoping it will dissipate on its own.

These are a few ways that dysfunction shows up in a family, unraveling the tapestry.

- Alcohol and drug abuse

- Other harmful addictions (i.e., sex, pornography)

- Sibling rivalry

- Financial issues

- Mental illness

- Divorce

- Incest/rape

- Abuse (physical, verbal, deception)

In the midst of dysfunction, individuals often question if they are the root cause of the issues. They may ponder why certain family members seem to have a problem with them or if their actions instigate conflicts. The abundance of family issues may even prompt many to wonder what is amiss within their family dynamics. Some may even comment, "What's wrong with my family? Why can't we find harmony?" Amid the turmoil, some family members may simply yearn for an end to the discord, hoping to cease the cycle of quarrels and disagreements. They envision the beautiful piece, the tapestry, the family.

"You don't choose family. They are God's gift to you,
as you are to them."
–Desmond Tutu

Definition of a Dysfunctional Family

According to the dictionary, dysfunction encompasses traits such as brokenness, flaws, deterioration, debilitation, and problems. Wikipedia describes a dysfunctional family as "One marked by conflict, misbehavior or abuse, where relationships among members are often tense and rife with neglect, yelling and screaming." In such families, individuals may feel compelled to endure negative treatment. Dysfunction stifles open dialogue and suppresses the freedom to express thoughts and feelings openly with the family dynamic.

Origins of Chaos

So, one might wonder, where did all this family chaos stuff first start ? Well, family dysfunction is first noted and displayed in the Holy Bible, with two brothers, Cain and Abel, the two sons of Adam and Eve. So yes, family dysfunction dates back over 6,000 years. In this story, dysfunction was present as sibling rivalry. It's noted that childhood feelings turned into resentment. Cain grows up to be a farmer and Abel becomes a shepherd. When these two brothers make sacrifices to God, He favors one over the other. Cain becomes jealous and murders Abel. Unfortunately, this becomes a long story in history that is still unbelievable today.

While no family is perfect, God desires for us to love one another and learn to get along. Despite individual differences that lead to family chaos, God can fix anything —no matter the hurt, pain, or issue. I believe healing begins when people dialogue. Communicate with your family. Lay it all out. We should not allow for family issues to lie dormant, hidden and continue throughout generations. Remember that Satan comes to steal, kill, and destroy. The devil wants to destroy families. Families can defeat this plan. Families, meaning all members, need to believe it is possible and work together. According to Mark 9:23 (NKJV), Jesus said to him, *"If you can believe, all things are possible to him who believes."*

A Common Thread

In the intricate tapestry of family life, dysfunction is a common thread found in all families. Dysfunction often involves complex interplays of individual choices and family dynamics. It lurks in the shadows, waiting to surface in unexpected ways. From the most affluent households to the humblest abodes, dysfunction is a silent companion, the common thread that weaves through the fabric of family relations. However, dysfunction is a phenomenon so prevalent that it often conceals itself behind closed doors and masks itself by societal expectations.

Within the tapestry is often discord and resentment, and in the intricate dance of family dynamics, dysfunction will eventually take center stage. No matter how strong the interwoven threads may seem, if allowed, it can and will destroy family relations for a lifetime. Furthermore, every family seems to harbor that one individual-catalyst of annoyance, negativity, and perpetual discord. These individuals, often unemployed yet mysteriously, are always donning new outfits at family functions. These individuals have mastered the art of deflecting blame onto others for the consequences of their decisions. It's a tragic cycle, a spiral of poor choices perpetuated by a refusal to take responsibility. The paradox of equal love, attention, and opportunities bestowed upon each family member is often marred by the bitterness of resentment. This narrative contends with the question: Why direct scornfulness toward a sibling who aligns with the best-laid plans? Equal opportunity was given to all. It's an urgent call to action, a proclamation that opportunities for transformation await those with the tenacity to seek a better path while other family members evade hard work while seeking the easy way out.

Some family members find solace in entitlement, expecting the world to cater to their every whim. Spoiled and indulged, they become recipients of a misguided form of love that backfires. The belief that constantly giving in to their desires will inspire hard work proves to be an illusion. Entitlement, like a poisonous seed, germinates and grows into a twisted sense of expectation. Karma, the great equalizer, whispers in the background, reminding us that every action has consequences. The world is a circle, and what goes around comes around. Yet despite these cosmic warnings, there are those who persist in believing that the universe owes them something. Sad but true, those who've received the most unearned assistance often end up squandering it, like water slipping through careless fingers. As dysfunction unfolds, the blame game commences. Should we blame the emotional unit that binds the family together? The matriarch? The patriarch?

We have all made a few poor life decisions. We have all had challenges we had to face, but don't allow that to become your excuse. No one is perfect, however, don't continue to make the same poor decisions. Perhaps you can begin with, stop spending money unnecessarily. Place all needs before any of your wants. Become a wise consumer. Ask yourself: How many clothes and shoes do I actually need? How much stuff is too much stuff? Especially when you've got it all in storage, anyway? Well, now you just found another way to save a few bucks. Get creative, use your God-given talents to take life to the next level. Try to minimize. Don't hate on another family member. Frugality doesn't have to last forever, but it sure can help you hold steady.

Ask yourself: Am I prepared for a life emergency? Can my family bury me if I die today? Will my family have to scrape together to bury me? Have I handled all of my business? Again, shame on you if you haven't even thought about these important issues. Don't allow someone else to have to carry your burden. Become responsible for yourself.

Navigating the Blame

Who truly bears the burden of dysfunction in the family? Who does the family blame for the dysfunction in the family? Is the matriarch at fault? Is it the patriarch's fault? Are Mom and Dad at the center of all the dysfunction? Sometimes it seems too complicated to understand. Perhaps the blame doesn't lie solely with these two figures. It's a collective responsibility. The family unit, as an emotional ecosystem, influences individual choices. According to Dr. Murray Bowen, who was an American psychiatrist, professor, and author of several books, The Family Systems Theory suggests that individuals cannot be understood in isolation from one another, but as a part of a family, as the family is an emotional unit. Dr. Murray Bowen says that the goal of any family system is to build into the individual relationships of each person in a way that breeds cooperation, respect, kindness, and love. Not all family members choose to take the same path of independence, stability, and success. "The trouble maker" emerges not in isolation but as a response to the family's shortcomings, a product of systemic issues that contribute to instability and dysfunction. But are these individuals really to blame? Or have the problems of the family contributed to certain individuals making the "bad" choices? In most families, everyone wants to place blame on the next person. No matter if you are the introvert or extrovert in the family, you still play a significant role in making up the family unit.

Dysfunction in the Face of Death

The death of a family member will further divide an already dysfunctional and separated family. The true extent of dysfunction becomes apparent when faced with death. Believe it or not, family arguments and physical altercations might break out while planning or during funeral services. Unfortunately, most of us have either heard of or have actually witnessed episodes of family drama. Yep.. That's right. At the Funeral. Major fallouts, actual fist fights, and arguments occur when a family member dies. Families experience high levels of stress, along with intensified tension, especially if it's the death of a mother "matriarch" or father "patriarch" of a family. Often these two individuals were the "glue" that was holding the already divided family together.

Grief, in combination with preplanning and financial issues, can and will often exacerbate any prior family issues. During these times, some members become more selfish. Everyone wants things done their way. No one really seems to want to compromise. According to Dr. Alejandra Vasquez, a certified grief counselor, favoritism also contributes to reasons families may struggle right before or after a death.

Not getting along or siblings taking sides is also a big problem when death occurs in the family. Often, this leaves out one or two siblings. Feelings of resentment and a belief that they are being "looked over" or bypassed are apparent.

Dysfunction Amid Holidays

Oh, no! It's the holidays.. Some of us really regret having to hang out during this time of year. I'd like to think that most people have dreaded or have had second thoughts about having to attend a holiday dinner with members of their own family. There's always the hesitation and thought of irritation when you know that a certain family member you don't care for will be present.

I'm sure that this idea of sharing a family holiday dinner can become quite stressful. Most individuals will most likely immediately conjure in their minds a preconceived negative notion of the special event or dinner. Many people perhaps even dread having to sit in the same room with certain family members. I'm sure that many individuals would even prefer to " sit this one out." Some people just ain't ready for all the drama. It's sad when you feel you can't even be with family without having to have crazy foolishness and family drama.

Unfortunately, many people have stated that many disagreements and arguments start before dinner can actually get on the plates. It's sad that the first disagreement can sometimes end the entire dinner. Family members storm out of the holiday celebration. Well, one might find it strange that sometimes the main argument is why a certain person's home was chosen as the place to hold the dinner or event. Siblings often argue and will make a bold statement up front to let others know that if the dinner is at the "wrong person's house, then I ain't even going." Forget it. This is sometimes an immediate reason to decline a family invitation.

All hell can break loose right there in front of other invited guests and children. From the outside looking in, it probably looks like something you'd see in a great Tyler Perry movie. A moment that might make you laugh, cry, and cuss all at the same time. Unbelievable moments occur in many homes. Unfortunately, during what should be a family moment of fun memories, sharing and caring, turns into an episodic and ridiculous kind of day. Moments like these only separate the family much further. Hurt that lasts for generations. Unfortunately, the children present hold these memories for years to come. Often, family members never get the apologies and forgiveness they want or so deserve.

Unveiling Family Secrets

Families keep their secrets within the family. These could be present issues or past events that are taboo to talk about. In some cultures, sharing family secrets with others to whom they don't belong to the family is a no-no. You simply don't do it. Some family secrets like incest, rape, marital affairs, physical abuse, drug abuse and many more are even kept hidden from those of the immediate family. I often think of the old saying, "What they don't know won't hurt anybody."

Families are often too ashamed or embarrassed to expose a family secret. People often judge or blame individuals who either share or do not share when they know information about hurtful family issues or events. Unfortunately, when people keep family secrets hidden, exposing them only causes an already dysfunctional family to be further torn apart. I believe that family secrets eventually surface regardless of how some try to hide them. As the old saying goes, "What's done in the dark comes to light." So, it's probably better to be open and honest with all family members. Yes, some may disagree and say, "What they don't know won't hurt them. For some may agree to just leave well enough alone. However, the individuals they hide information from hurt more when they learn of these secrets. These hidden secrets only cause more strife. Sad to realize that there is no way of actually changing the outcome. We all might sit and wonder, why do some family members continue to disregard family secrets? While some family members have been fully aware of the rumors that have come out for many years.

Jealousy, Envy, and Deceit

Jealousy, as it is defined, means *feeling or showing envy of someone or their achievements and advantages*. Unfortunately, jealousy exists in every family. According to James 3:16 (KJV), *"For where envying and strife is, there is confusion and every evil works."* I often sit and wonder why jealousy exists. Especially in one's own family. I question if jealousy exists because the natural side of our beings just always wants what other individuals have.

Why do people like to tear others down? Why are some people envious of others who have worked hard for what they have? Often, people show this through their material possessions. Most times, at least one person in every family is envious of the achievements of other family members. Why hate? Why be bitter? Why be envious? Hard work can equal success, at some point, therefore achievement can be for anyone who will work hard enough to get it. Some people work hard, and honestly, some will stop at nothing until they pursue their goals. Does jealousy build over time? Does jealousy turn into hate? For many family members, it might feel as though jealousy builds. It may even feel as though jealousy makes loved ones hateful, hurtful and deceitful. It's unfortunate, but I'm sure many people have heard of family instances where bald-faced lies are told in order to ruin another family member's character and reputation. We must remember that God is in control of the situation. As it states in Romans 8:31(KJV), *"What then shall we say in response to these things?"* If God is for us, who can be against us? According to Isaiah 54:17 (KJV), *"No weapon formed against you shall prosper."*

Keep your head up. Keep your integrity. Satan intentionally tries to disturb your peace. Remember that unhappy people envy you for a reason. Yep, your haters. They see you as being great. It's just something about you they wish they had. Don't allow jealous family members to make you stoop down to their level. Perhaps they are suffering from low self-esteem. Good character and integrity are qualities that are built over time. Life qualities that just speak for themselves. A person's life speaks for itself. Truth prevails all the time. Other individuals affiliated with the family will even take notice of what is or isn't. No sides are taken. As the scripture says in Exodus 14:14(KJV), *"The Lord will fight for you, and you shall hold your peace."* Remember to continue to fast and pray for family members that continue to despise you.

Although sometimes it may seem as if there is no end in sight, hold on to what the word says. God's got you. Stay faithful, for soon a change will come. Learning to be the bigger person does not come easy. Keeping your dignity, class, and great character will be so much better in the end.

What Does Birth Order Got to Do With It?

Does it matter if you were born into your family as a first, second, or last child? I often heard individuals brag about the order in which they were born into their families. Many seem to be happy about being the firstborn, which makes them the oldest child. Some say middle children are "special," while, of course, some are content with being the last or youngest child in the family.

So many myths seem to be placed on birth order and birth rights in families. Myths such as "I'm the oldest child, therefore I have more to say about making family decisions." There are also myths that suggest that a middle child in a family seems to turn out to be the "black sheep" of the family or the "problem child." Many notions support the myth that this child possibly received less time with their parents when compared to that of the oldest or younger sibling. There are also myths that middle children are usually not high achievers. These myths are exactly what they are, just coincidental to some. Many people frown about the myth of the youngest child. Naysayers have suggested that this child is the most spoiled. Many seem to think that parents put more time and energy into this child. Parents perhaps know that this is their last chance to participate in school activities and such.

Unfortunately, constant myths and accusations will always surround birth order. These accusations often surface in family discussions, especially about the "baby of the family" who always seems to get everything they want. Some siblings might even feel like they get "more chances," "more love," "more patience," "more guidance," and "less responsibility."

I believe every child raised in the same household turns out differently. Each child has their own personalities, identities and experiences. We cannot place all children in the same box. Parents should make sure that every child and all siblings feel equally loved. It is important not to give preferential treatment to one particular child. I think that even when children grow into adults, all siblings should have equal rights when it comes down to making family decisions regarding aging or sick parents. We should define a person by their integrity and character, not only by the order in which they were born. Good morals stand out and stand up. Stability and responsibility usually go together. Bossy family members should not intimidate other siblings. It is never acceptable to intimidate or force someone solely based on their birth order. All family members should have the same entitlements. Birth order should never be the determining factor for family relations.

Birth order means just that, the order in which you were born and nothing else. Birth order should never place an emphasis on how and when family members communicate. Hierarchy should not matter. No family member should feel as if they have authority over another sibling. We need to put an immediate stop to false thinking and the idealization of power. Parents, please intervene. The dysfunction will only continue and expand if you don't. Who cares which order you were born in if you didn't get your life together? If everyone is grown and on their own, then surely they can have a say when it comes to family issues. My problem is, how can an individual "lead family" when they have not even learned the rules of life as a follower? Why do some siblings continue to hate and bother other siblings about nonsense and drama? Could it be that this person has not yet really achieved what they have always wanted in life?

Psychologist Frank Sulloway's theory on birth order suggests that firstborns who are physically superior to their siblings at a young age are more likely to show dominant behavior and therefore become less agreeable. He also suggested that competition between siblings for parental investment leads children to cultivate family niches that are associated with birth order. The first born receive greater investment from their parents and have their pick of niches within the family system. Alfred Adler, who was an Austrian medical doctor and psychotherapist, suggested the order in which you were born in your family affects your personality. Adler suggested that although children may be born into the same household, their birth order greatly influences their psychological development. He also stated that different positions in a family birth order may be correlated to both positive and negative life outcomes. Adler stated that the youngest children tend to be more ambitious while middle children are optimally positioned in the family and are characterized by emotional stability.

Caring for Aging Parents

As we grow older, become adults and form our own families, our parents too are growing older. Again, just think about how many times you have seen or heard that children and parents exchange rolls. The tables turn. Parents who once took care of us now require for someone to take care of them. The aging process is no joke. While many take it lightly, growing old is inevitable. While there seem to be many temporary remedies to help maintain a youthful look, unfortunately nothing will change a person's chronological age. As time shows us wrinkles, hair loss, joint pains, memory loss and slower movement just happen. The aging process will force you to take notice of the changes in ourselves as well as with our parents. Do you remember when your mom or dad would cook and clean? Maybe drive to the grocery store, pick up the laundry or simply go visit with family and friends.

Unfortunately, as our parents age, these tasks become minimized, and some even come to a complete stop. No longer can they operate simple chores and tasks by themselves. Caring for our elderly parents is not a tea party. It can become overwhelming and taxing. It's like having a second job that you must do. Why is the job of caring for the elderly so overwhelming some might ask? Well, some have stated that caring for your own children, along with dealing with marital issues and maintaining a job is time consuming. There is just never any real time for oneself. Caring for an elderly parent is a process that you should share with other family members. All siblings should play a part in the journey of caring for an elderly parent. This job is much too hard to bear alone if there are others that can assist. Unfortunately, many have to do it alone. Even despite your personal lives. It's kinda like this: either you do it, or you pay someone else to do it.

There are several options. Dementia and Alzheimer's are the aging diseases of many elderly individuals. These diseases are sometimes debilitating and alter a person's complete life. It leaves our loved ones unable to remember and function as they once did. The changes in an aging parent affect most families negatively. It can bring about more dysfunction in an already broken family. Just the fact alone that Mom and Dad are no longer who they used to be is quite difficult to accept. Although it's no one's fault in particular, I believe that it's just God's way of how life sometimes happens.

Caretaking is a full-time responsibility. It can sometimes mean going as far as placing Mom or Dad into a senior living facility. It can even mean moving an elderly parent into your residence. Another option could be to rotate and take turns with each child sharing in the care of their aging parent. Does sharing the care for aging parents cause dysfunction? Yes. Especially when siblings refuse to assist, or they simply cannot take part in the process. Why is caring for an aging parent so stressful? Often, we are tired from our own business and life affairs. Most people barely have time for their own issues, let alone someone else's. This process of sharing in the care of an aging parent has to be worked out. Regardless of other life duties and responsibilities, sacrifices must be made.

Now, there's always going to be at least one family member who can't assist with caretaking. Unfortunately, this often brings more burden on the family. Chaos erupts and brings more division into an already torn family. My suggestion is to communicate and plan a strategy. Flexibility will become important during this time. Everyone involved will need to look at the whole picture. Here are some questions to ask: What does our elderly parent want for his or her long-term care? Are all affairs in order? Questions like these will always be important to ask an aging parent before memory loss takes place. It's important to take care of business before the parent gets to a stage in life where they can no longer answer and care for themselves.

Well, trust and believe, differences in understandings will be "misunderstood" and this can sometimes start a family argument and sometimes a physical confrontation between family members. It will be important to remember that lots of love, patience, prayer, and respect for others must be present. Again, this is not the time to be selfish. While this will be hard at times, just keep in mind that you are all doing what is best and most economically fit for your aging parent. Sometimes the lack of financial resources in caring for the aging parent will bring about division. So, this could mean redirecting assets, minimizing personal possessions, etc. Not having enough money to care for the aging parent can only make things worse and stressful for everyone in the family. With a lack of money, yet everyone has to work together on doing what is best for the parent. It will hurt to see the sale of the family home, but if this is the best way of caring for an aging parent, then so be it. It is what it is, and sometimes there is no better way.

Navigating Family Illnesses

Physical illness, mental illnesses, and any sickness or disease can become a hardship for any family. When our loved ones get sick, everyone in the family has to make adjustments. Regardless of whether it's Mom, Dad, or children, taking care of others can quickly become overwhelming. It demands a significant amount of time, energy, and emotional investment, often leading to complete burnout. Both short term and long-term care requires that everyone jump right in to assist. This is necessary, so that no one family member ends up having a physical or mental breakdown themselves.

Most family members don't like the role of "caretaker" somebody's gotta do it. Not everyone wants to be a "nurse." If families share the responsibility of caretaking, it prevents one person from bearing the entire weight, which causes a lot of undue stress. It's very important for caretakers to remember that caretakers need self-care. Don't forget about yourselves.

Mental illness is real. It can destroy the family system. Illnesses like bipolar, anxiety, panic attacks, PTSD, schizophrenia, depression, alcoholism, and drug abuse all affect the mind. These issues can become a family's worst nightmare.

The redundancy of mental breakdowns and outrageous episodes will soon take a toll on the family, causing family trauma and instability. Whenever a family member reverts to hurting themselves, hurting others, stealing from loved ones, lying, and perhaps killing, all to maintain mental stability, is definitely a major problem. Mental illness is too serious to be ignored.

Perhaps you are the parent of a child with a mental disorder. Whatever you do, please do not blame yourself for allowing something like this to happen. This is not your fault. With suicide, if a young child takes their life, parents and family members often find themselves thinking about what they missed. Was there not enough time being spent with this child? Why? So many parents and other family members struggle with these questions. It's unfortunate when death by suicide occurs in the family. It's unbelievable that individuals find it too difficult to fight their demons, which are tormenting them. Suicide, unfortunately, is a loss that some parents and siblings never heal from. Some individuals may even grieve for a lifetime. Although the memory of losing a loved one will always remain in the minds of everyone, remember that God is able to mend a broken heart. According to Psalms 147:30 (KJV), *"He heals the broken-hearted and binds up their wounds."*

Mental health requires a family to seek professional help. You might think you can, but you really can't do it alone. Family members with mental health issues need lots of support. Lots of love, patience, consistency, and understanding is required. Although the care for these such members can become unbelievable, don't give up on them because, believe it or not, God can heal the mind. Continue to seek help from outside interventions, like doctors, counselors, clergy, and specialized therapists. It's also good that the caretaker and other family members find a support group. Physical illnesses can deplete all family members. When there is someone in the family who solely depends on someone to do everything for them, it can become depressing. Providing care for someone who cannot do things independently becomes challenging. Simple tasks that we take for granted in our daily lives, like eating, walking, talking, or using the bathroom, become significant responsibilities. These tasks alone can become challenging and depressing for all parties involved.

I believe everyone will get back whatever you give. If you help your parents, guess what? Someone will help you when you need it. Karma. Yep, you just wait and see. It all comes back. After all, nothing compares to giving love to the person responsible for bringing you into this world.

The Religious Divide

Well hat do you do when your family has different religious beliefs? What's the family's attitude when you don't attend a family wedding, baptism or christening?

Should religious divides keep families apart? Unfortunately, families often miss out on treasured moments and memories that last a lifetime because of religious beliefs and unbelief. Today, the world has over 4,000 religions, many of which are made up of churches, congregations, tribes, faith groups, movements, and cultures. Although Christianity is the largest religion in the United States, not everyone takes part in it. Should religion be a reason families can no longer get together at holidays or other family gatherings? Regardless of what religion your family associates with, even if you disagree, that should not be the reason families never come together.

We should respect everyone's religious beliefs. Everyone has a right to choose. Does this mean that siblings or cousins cannot visit each other's home? It's sad to place this type of pressure on family members. The burden of not being together, just because we don't agree about the Bible or the Quran. Just because siblings grow up learning a certain religion doesn't mean that they will stay in it. Just because Grandma and Grandpa believed in it, doesn't mean that it has to be forced on future generations. While practicing the same religion seems to be a great idea for the entire family, generationally speaking, in most cultures, it's almost expected that siblings and children follow what and how mom and dad did it. Family members who do not adhere to this norm of the traditional religion are often perceived as stubborn and difficult to handle. Unfortunately, as children grow into adults and build their own families, many grow apart, some will even seek new faith groups. Breaking tradition and even sometimes thought of as "weirdos." Regardless of this matter, I feel like religious differences should never divide families. Keeping loved one's apart for months and years. We need to put our differences aside and love our families. The world needs more love. Families must learn to rise above the religious divide. It's okay. Love comes first.

Family Politics

Politics and family dysfunction are very similar. Kind of like Democrats versus Republicans. Kind of like oil and water. Like ketchup and pancakes. They are not compatible. Not caring for or liking one party will always take center stage. Arguing or always being in opposition to one another takes a considerable amount of energy. Energy that could be used for other things.

There will always be two sides, individuals who never seem to want to agree. Unfortunately, just like some egotistical politicians who never give in to what is right, so are family members in dysfunction. God made us all so different, unique in our own beings. Yep, believe it or not, God designed us this way. It's okay that we each hold our own opinions and beliefs, and just like politics, family dysfunction sometimes goes overlooked by many for years.

For many, ignoring family issues then comes to the forefront, just like a gigantic explosion. It will get everyone's attention. The kind that you can't help but stop and deal with. That is because now you have to. When a family can no longer avoid having the "family discussion," unfortunately dysfunction, just as in politics, will leave some families feeling as though we won, while others feel as if they lost. It's kinda like the more you talk about a situation, the worse it makes you feel. Some even feel like if you ignore it will simply go away. It makes you feel as though a change will never come. Although it's tough to take sides some family members do. It's like they took an unofficial vote. Taking sides, which really never makes the family issue any better. The chaos just continues, repeating itself with a never-ending cycle.

Families must learn to get along. Work out your differences. Do it for the sake of the next family generation. Take a stand, but continue to work for progress. For in time, change will come.

Conclusion

In summary, the emergence of dysfunction within a family does not negate the love existing among its members. Instead, it often reflects their collective efforts to navigate and manage family challenges. Dysfunction, although perceived as disruptive, can paradoxically serve as a mechanism for maintaining the family system. Yet, it is imperative to acknowledge that dysfunction may also veil deeper underlying family issues, causing genuine introspection and proactive resolution to foster healthier family dynamics.

It's essential to recognize that God's love encompasses families, desiring for them to thrive and experience abundant life. God's ideal for families involves harmony, devoid of drama, arguments, or conflicts. As stated in Romans 12:18 *"If it be possible as much as lieth in you, live peaceably with all men."* Embracing God's example, we strive to cultivate love in our hearts and pursue unity among family members. Conversely, the adversary seeks to sow discord and dismantle family bonds. Satan thrives on brokenness, striving to sow division and chaos, as stated in John 10:10, *"The thief cometh not, but for to steal and to kill, and to destroy.* " Resisting Satan's influence, we must refuse to let him triumph. Instead, we extend love even to those deemed "problematic", knowing that love has the power to overcome most obstacles. Don't let dysfunction prevail: rather, let love guide our actions and strengthen your family bonds.

Family Tree

Make a list of your family members.

Parents:

____

____

____

Siblings:

____

____

____

____

Children:

____

____

____

Stepchildren:

____

____

____

Grandchildren:

____

____

____

____

Spouse's Parents:

____

____

____

____

Spouse's Children:

____

____

____

____

Spouse's Siblings:

____

____

____

____

Essential Documents Every Family Shoud Possess

1. **Trust or Will**: Having a legally binding document outlining how assets and property should be distributed upon death is crucial for ensuring the wishes of the deceased are honored and avoiding potential disputes among family members.

2. **Power of Attorney**: Establishing powers of attorney for both health care and financial matters is essential. This allows designated individuals to make decisions on behalf of the person if they become unable to do so themselves due to illness or incapacity, ensuring their affairs are managed according to their preferences.

3. **Life Insurance or Burial Insurance Policies**: Securing life insurance or burial insurance policies provides financial protection for loved ones in the event of the policyholder's death. These policies can help cover funeral expenses, outstanding debts, and provide financial support for dependents, offering peace of mind during difficult times.

In addition to these documents, families may also benefit from having advance directives, such as living wills and healthcare proxies, to outline preferences for medical treatment and end-of-life care. It's important to regularly review and update these documents as circumstances change to ensure they accurately reflect the family's wishes and circumstances.

Notes

41

A Prayer to Pray

Lord help me to become a better family member to my family.

Lord help me to become a better daughter to my parents, a better mother to my children, a better father to my son.

Lord open up my heart and mind, help me to understand the chaos, hurt, lies, deceit and family secrets. Some of these issues have tormented my family for much too long.

Lord while no family is perfect, God, I know that you are able to do anything. For you have proven to be a non failing God.

Lord elevate my mind, grant me more patience, hope and courage.

Lord for I believe and trust that you can and will help us to make it all right. For things will get better.

Lord, I'm taking one step at a time. I will allow you to take control.

AMEN.

www.ingramcontent.com/pod-product-compliance
Lightning Source LLC
Chambersburg PA
CBHW021327160726
47994CB00004B/1644